Lost Railways of Co. Antrim

by
Stephen Johnson

The former Ballymena & Larne narrow gauge locomotive No. 109 stands at Ballyboley with the 6.28 p.m. departure to Doagh, August 1930. Built in 1880 by Beyer, Peacock, this 2-6-0ST was renumbered by the Belfast & Northern Counties Railway in 1897 and survived until 1934.

ACKNOWLEDGEMENTS
The publishers wish to thank the following for contributing pictures to this book: John Alsop for the front cover and pages 22, 26, 32 and 35; R.M. Casserley for pages 1, 3, 5–10, 12–15, 18–21, 23–25, 27–29, 36, 39, and 42–48 (with the exceptions of those on pages 14, and 42–44, all of these photographs were taken by H.C. Casserley); Ian McCullough for the inside front cover, pages 2, 4, 11, 17, 30, 33 and the back cover; and Des Quail for pages 16, 31, 34, 37, 38 and 41. The publishers supplied the pictures on page 40 and the inside back cover.

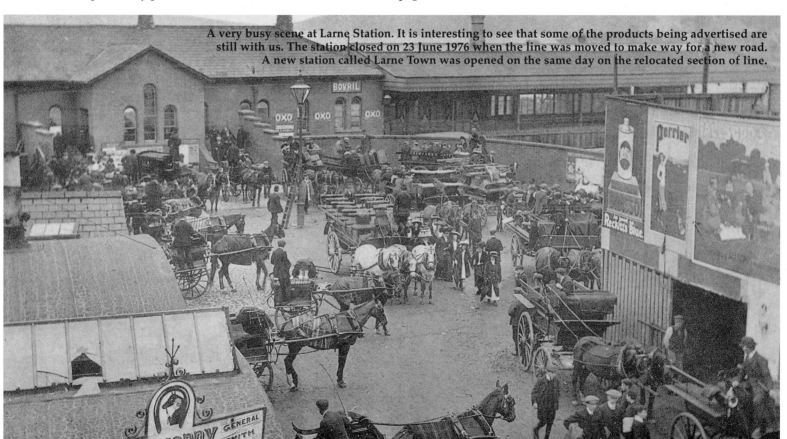

A very busy scene at Larne Station. It is interesting to see that some of the products being advertised are still with us. The station closed on 23 June 1976 when the line was moved to make way for a new road. A new station called Larne Town was opened on the same day on the relocated section of line.

INTRODUCTION

In looking at the railways of Co. Antrim, the most noticeable aspect is the dominance of the NCC, or Northern Counties Committee, which owned nearly all the lines in the county. The NCC started off as a subsidiary of the English Midland Railway when they acquired the Belfast & Northern Counties Railway in 1903. With the English grouping of railway companies in 1923, the Midland Railway became part of the London, Midland & Scottish Railway (LMS) and so did the NCC.

The LMS influence became quite noticeable in the county. A number of locomotives and carriages were built at Derby and transported to Ireland. The NCC W Class bear more than passing resemblance to the LMS Ivatt Moguls whereas the WT Class 2-6-4T are very similar to the Fairburn and Stanier 2-6-4Ts. Two 0-6-0T 3Fs, or 'Jinty's', were re-gauged and became the NCC Class Y. Following severe war damage, forty-four LMS carriages were re-gauged and sent to Ireland to alleviate the rolling stock shortage.

When the 'big four' railway companies in Britain were nationalised in 1948, the LMS and other companies ceased to exist, being replaced by British Railways which was administered by the Railway Executive of the British Transport Commission. However, the NCC continued as a separate region of the Railway Executive for the time being while a complex bill was steered through Parliament to set up what would become known as the Ulster Transport Authority. This was a public corporation with compulsory powers to acquire road and rail operations and to provide an economical and integrated system of public transport for passengers and goods in Northern Ireland. The new concern came into force on 1 October 1948, acquiring the Belfast & County Down Railway and the Northern Ireland Road Transport Board. The NCC remained independent until an agreement was made for it to merge with the UTA in December 1948, an arrangement which formally came into force on 1 April 1949.

Unfortunately, it didn't take too long before things started to go wrong for the railways under the UTA. The closure of stations and complete railway lines soon started and it became obvious that road transport was being developed at the expense of the railways. By 1965 the situation was becoming critical and it became clear that the UTA was in trouble. A new concern, the Northern Ireland Transport Holding Company, was set up, with the railways coming under the control of Northern Ireland Railways in April 1968. This company runs the few remaining lines still open in Co. Antrim – the former Belfast & Northern Counties route to Londonderry via Coleraine, the branch to Portrush, and the busy commuter line to Larne via Carrickfergus.

Unlike the NCC, the other railway concern in Co. Antrim managed to remain independent to the end. This was the pioneering Giant's Causeway, Portrush & Bush Valley Tramway Company. Built to connect the small town of Bushmills, famous for its whiskey production, to the growing railway network, it also provided a link for tourists visiting the geological wonder known as the Giant's Causeway. From the start the tramway was to be powered by electricity. A hydroelectric power station was constructed to supply the traction current, making it the first hydroelectrically powered tramway in the world. It survived until 1949 when falling income and the need for refurbishment forced it to close. On a happier note, a group of enthusiasts have formed the Giant's Causeway Railway, relaying part of the tramway between Bushmills and the Giant's Causeway. Using locomotives and carriages from the Shane's Castle Railway, one can again enjoy a ride along this unique route.

This book starts by looking at the broad gauge lines of Co. Antrim with the branches to Ballyclare and Randalstown. The narrow gauge lines centred around Ballymena come next, followed by the Ballycastle Railway, a narrow gauge concern that managed to outlast all others in the county. The Giant's Causeway Tramway is last before looking at some of the closed stations on the lines still operating in Co. Antrim.

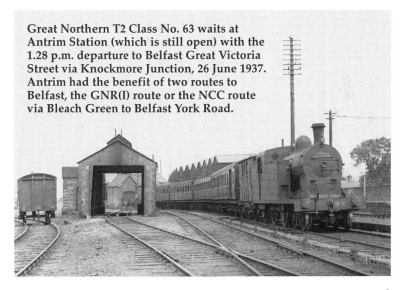

Great Northern T2 Class No. 63 waits at Antrim Station (which is still open) with the 1.28 p.m. departure to Belfast Great Victoria Street via Knockmore Junction, 26 June 1937. Antrim had the benefit of two routes to Belfast, the GNR(I) route or the NCC route via Bleach Green to Belfast York Road.

Ballyclare Junction – Ballyclare

Passenger service withdrawn	1 January 1938		*Stations closed*	*Date*
Distance	4.5 miles		Kings Moss Halt	1 January 1938
Company	Northern Counties Committee		Lisnalinchy	1 January 1938
			Lisnalinchy Racecourse	1950
Stations closed	*Date*		Ballyclare	1 January 1938
Ballyclare Junction *	4 December 1961			

The entrance to Ballyclare broad gauge station. This station was the terminus of the Belfast & Northern Counties broad gauge branch to the town. Opened in 1884, the station lost its regular passenger service in 1938.

* Formerly named Ballynure Road and renamed Ballyclare Junction on 3 November 1884 with the opening of the branch. As Ballynure Road, the station was closed between August 1875 and June 1877.

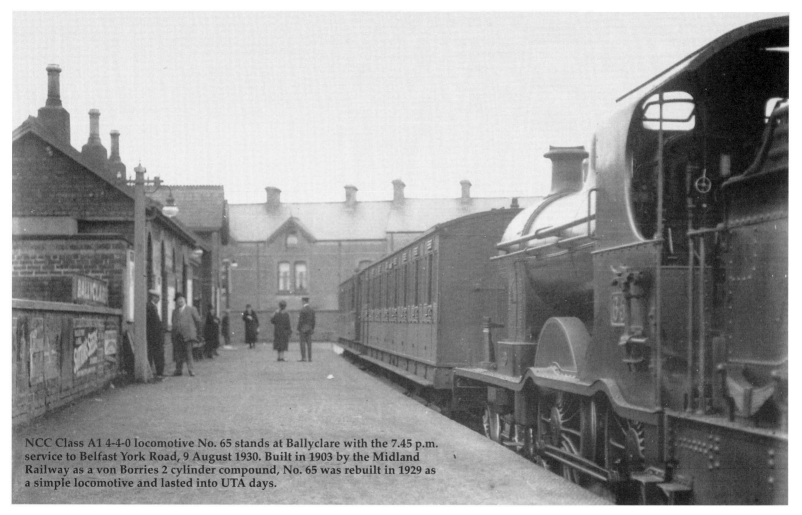

NCC Class A1 4-4-0 locomotive No. 65 stands at Ballyclare with the 7.45 p.m. service to Belfast York Road, 9 August 1930. Built in 1903 by the Midland Railway as a von Borries 2 cylinder compound, No. 65 was rebuilt in 1929 as a simple locomotive and lasted into UTA days.

During the late nineteenth century, the town of Ballyclare was the centre of the paper mill industry in Ireland. This fact had not been overlooked by the Belfast & Northern Counties Railway and in 1881 and 1882 the BNCR obtained Acts to build a branch from their main Belfast–Londonderry line. The branch left the main line one mile to the west of Ballynure Road Station at Kingsbog Junction and opened on 3 November 1884. Upon the opening of the line, Ballynure Road Station was renamed Ballyclare Junction.

Railcar No. 1 at Ballyclare, 13 May 1950. This railcar was built at York Road Works in 1933 and was powered by two Leyland petrol engines and had a hydraulic transmission. No. 1 is now preserved by the RPSI at Whitehead.

The line ran the three and a half miles from the junction to the town of Ballyclare, climbing sharply to 358 feet above sea level, the highest point on the entire NCC broad gauge, before falling gradually to the terminus. In 1885 a new station one mile onto the branch at Lisnalinchy was opened. The hoped for traffic never came up to expectations, but an attempt to stimulate trade was made in 1926 with the opening of Kings Moss Halt and in 1934 with the opening of Lisnalinchy Racecourse Station on racedays only. The end came on 1 January 1938 with the cessation of passenger trains. Goods traffic survived a few more months until 2 May. That would have been the end of the story had it not been for the Second World War. The line was reopened and worked as a siding in 1940 to serve an army depot at Ballyclare and it survived for another ten years. Lisnalinchy Racecourse Station remained open for race day traffic only until 1950, when the Ulster Transport Authority finally closed the whole line. Ballyclare Junction Station, which was on the main line, remained open to passenger trains until 4 December 1961.

Cookstown Junction – Toome Bridge

		Stations closed	Date
Passenger service withdrawn	28 August 1950	Randalstown (old station)	10 November 1856
Distance	11.5 miles	Randalstown (new station)	28 August 1950
Company	Northern Counties Committee	Randalstown Military Platform	Date unknown
		Staffordstown (old station)	March 1864
Stations closed	*Date*	Staffordstown (new station)	28th August 1950
Cookstown Junction *	18 October 1976	Toome Bridge	28th August 1950

Cookstown Junction Station, facing Belfast, 20 June 1938. Opened in 1848 as Drumsough, the station was renamed in 1856 with the opening of the extension of the Randalstown branch to Cookstown. The branch lost its passenger service in 1950, but it took until April 1976 before the name reverted back to Drumsough, six months before it closed.

Built by the Belfast & Ballymena Railway, the branch to Randalstown was intended to make a link to a much grander scheme. On 3 August 1846, the Dublin, Belfast & Coleraine Junction Railway was incorporated with the intention of building a line from Armagh through Dungannon, Cookstown, Magherafelt, Ballymoney, Coleraine and Portstewart, terminating at Portrush. The B&BR were keen to get a connection into this scheme and submitted a bill in 1845 to make a branch to Randalstown from Drumsough on the Belfast to Ballymena line. The bill received Royal Assent on 21 July 1845 and work started in early 1846 with the line opening on 12 April 1848. However, the neighbouring DB&CJR had not yet started work and their land acquisition powers expired in 1849. Nothing more was heard of the scheme and the Belfast & Ballymena Railway were left with a fairly useless branch to Randalstown.

* Formerly known as Drumsough and renamed Cookstown Junction on 10 November 1856. It was renamed Drumsough once more from 26 April 1976.

Cookstown Junction again, this time with NCC locomotive No. 57, 'Galgorm Castle', in charge of the 5 p.m. service to Coleraine via the Derry Central line, 2 June 1938.

The B&BR were still keen to reach Cookstown and in 1851 a new proposal was made to extend the Randalstown branch to Cookstown via Toome Bridge and Magherafelt. A bill was duly lodged and became law in June 1853. However, work did not start until 1855 and the line was opened on 10 November 1856. The branch left the main Belfast to Ballymena line at Drumsough, which was renamed Cookstown Junction on the opening of the branch. The line climbed a little to Doyle's Bridge before descending the final mile into Randalstown Station on the east bank of the River Maine. Unfortunately, the main part of the town was on the other side of the river. The Cookstown extension crossed the River Maine on an impressive eight arch stone viaduct. The viaduct exists to this day, but the opportunity of resiting Randalstown Station was not taken. Instead, a new through station was built on the other side of a level crossing from the original terminus, opening the same day as the extension. However, the First World War did see Randalstown Military Platform being built on the other side of the viaduct in 1914.

The shed at Cookstown Junction, 20 June 1938. In the background is NCC locomotive No. 2, 'Glendun', a 4-4-0 built by the NCC in 1924.

The line then climbed again for a couple of miles before dropping down the three miles into Staffordstown. A new station, built in March 1864 replaced the original station there, the new station being a half mile to the east of the old one. From Staffordstown, the line continued to fall, running within sight of Lough Neagh to Toome Bridge. At Toome Bridge, a short line ran down to a wharf which dealt with sand and clay traffic. Leaving Toome Bridge Station, the line crossed the Lower Bann river by means of the Carlisle Bridge into Co. Derry. The Carlisle Bridge, named after the Earl of Carlisle, the then Lord Lieutenant of Ireland, was a lattice girder bridge with a centre opening span to allow shipping to pass. The B&BR became part of the Belfast & Northern Counties Railway on 15 May 1860 and subsequently part of the Midland Railway on 21 July 1903. The line finally closed to passengers on 28 August 1950. Freight services survived for another nine years before the Ulster Transport Authority finally closed the line on 5 October 1959. Cookstown Junction Station was finally renamed Drumsough on 26 April 1976 before it too closed just a few months later.

Ballymena – Larne Harbour

Passenger service withdrawn	1 June 1932 (Larne to Larne Harbour) / 1 February 1933 (Larne to Ballymena)		
Distance	25.5 miles		
Company	Northern Counties Committee		

Stations closed	*Date*
Ballymena Harryville *	1 January 1890
Kells	1 February 1933
Moorfields **	1 February 1933

Stations closed	*Date*
Collin Halt	1 February 1933
Ballynashee ***	1 February 1933
Ballyeaston Halt ****	1 February 1933
Ballyboley Junction *****	1 February 1933
Headwood †	1 February 1933
Kilwaughter Halt ††	1 February 1933
Larne	1 February 1933
Larne Harbour (new station) †††	1 June 1932
Larne Harbour (old station)	c.1890

NCC narrow gauge locomotive No. 113, a 2-4-2T von Borries 2 cylinder compound, makes its way between Larne Harbour and Larne next to the broad gauge line, 22 June 1937.

* Harryville remained in use for goods traffic and the 6.15 a.m. daily passenger service departure until September 1916.
** Opened 14 December 1882.
*** Opened 1879.
**** Opened in 1880 as Ballyeaston Bridge and closed on 1 June 1882. Reopened as Ballyeaston Halt in 1911.
***** Opened as Ballyclare Junction and renamed in 1889.
† Opened on 1 June 1882 as Ballygowan but was renamed Headwood from October 1882.
†† Opened in 1885 but was closed between March 1888 and January 1908.
††† Closed to narrow gauge services on 1 June 1932, this station remains open for broad gauge services.

Larne narrow gauge station seems to be the attention of some maintenance work in this view looking south.

The harbour at Larne had been home to the Stranraer to Larne steamer service since 1862. Not surprisingly, a number of schemes had been floated to link Larne to Londonderry and the north-west with a more direct route than the Belfast & Northern Counties circuitous route via Carrickfergus Junction. The successful company was the Ballymena & Larne Railway who had originally proposed a broad gauge line from Larne to Antrim in 1872. However, while in Parliament, the company withdrew the bill and submitted a second, less ambitious proposal. The Larne & Ballyclare Railway was duly incorporated to build a narrow gauge line from Larne to Ballyclare. Ballyclare had long been a centre for the papermaking industry, producing some fifty tons per week. The line received royal assent on 5 August 1873. However, the company was soon considering an extension to Ballymena as ore traffic from the north Antrim hills running into Ballymena on the three feet gauge Cushendall line promised to significantly increase profits. The proposed extension to Ballymena was to leave the Larne & Ballyclare Railway near Ballynure and terminate at Harryville on the southern side of Ballymena. Another line was envisaged to run from Harryville to connect with the Ballymena, Cushandall & Red Bay Railway, thus making the connection to the hoped for ore traffic. A bill was duly submitted to Parliament and passed on 7 August 1874. The Act incorporated the Ballymena & Larne Railway as a replacement for the Larne & Ballyclare Railway and authorised the new company to construct the two extensions. In the event, the connection from Harryville to the Cushendall line was not built in the form originally proposed. Lack of capital meant that work did not begin until 1876.

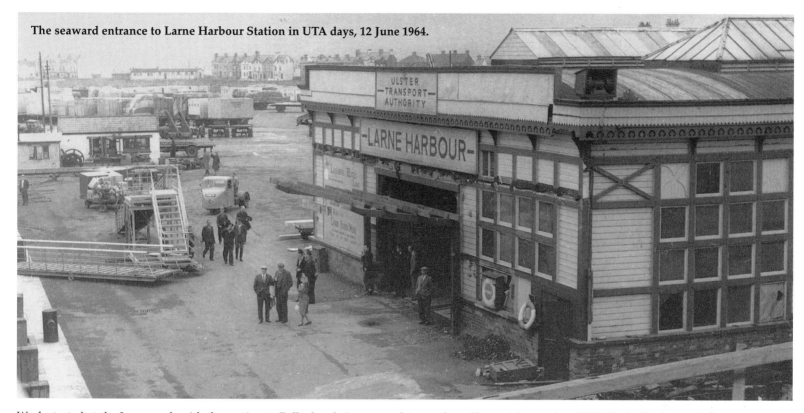

The seaward entrance to Larne Harbour Station in UTA days, 12 June 1964.

Work started at the Larne end, with the section to Ballyclare being opened to goods traffic on 1 September 1877. The Ballyclare to Ballymena section took a little longer and was opened to goods traffic on 1 June 1878. Following an inspection by the Board of Trade, the whole line was opened to passenger traffic on 24 August 1878. The terminus at Ballymena was at Harryville, a half mile short of the Belfast & Northern Counties station at Ballymena. The Ballymena & Larne Railway approached Parliament with another bill for eight extension railways in 1877. Three of these were authorised on 8 August 1878 – a branch to Doagh, another branch to Kilwaughter, which was never built, and a link line from Harryville to the BNCR station in Ballymena. Work on the Ballymena extension, known as the 'high level line', was duly completed and the link opened on 22 September 1880. The old Harryville terminus remained in use for a further ten years until 1 September 1890, and beyond that was still used for goods traffic and the 6.15 a.m. morning passenger departure each day until September 1916. In reaching the BNCR station at Ballymena, the B&LR connected to another narrow gauge line, the Ballymena, Cushendall & Red Bay Railway. The opening of the link allowed the direct conveyance of ore from the Cushendall line to Larne without trans-shipment as well as a cross platform interchange for Londonderry passengers catching the boat. However, the fortunes of the B&LR were not good; a hard winter of 1880 decimated income and there were no through bookings to Larne Harbour thanks to the B&NCR. Ore traffic diminished, with some of it reaching Larne by the longer broad gauge route of the BNCR.

UTA 2-6-4T Class WT No. 51 stands at Larne Harbour Station, 15 April 1953. No. 51 was built by British Railways at Derby in 1949 and was one of the last steam locomotives to work in regular service in the United Kingdom, being withdrawn by NIR in 1971.

Despite cutbacks, the company found the going increasingly difficult and tried to effect further economies by withdrawing the special boat trains! The final straw came when the Ballyclare Paper Mill asked for a reduction in carriage rates for raw materials. Running costs then started to exceed income and the company had no other option but to sell the line. This they did on 16 July 1889 when the Ballymena & Larne Railway became part of the Belfast & Northern Counties Railway. Having taken over the line, the BNCR decided to improve the route and its services. A new station at Larne Harbour was built and opened in 1890. The station had a double faced platform serving the narrow gauge on one side and the broad gauge on the other. Ballymena Station was rebuilt and completed in 1904, with special attention paid to the interchange between the broad gauge and narrow gauge boat trains. New locomotives of the compound type were built in 1892 and in 1928 the LMS NCC built four corridor bogie carriages complete with lavatories. But despite all these improvements, the end came with the 1933 railway strike which finished all passenger services on 1 February that year. The narrow gauge services had been discontinued between Larne and Larne Harbour on 1 June 1932 to allow the rebuilding of the harbour station. The Ballymena to Ballyboley Junction section closed completely on 2 June 1940. The remaining section from Larne Harbour to Ballyboley Junction and from there down the branch to Ballyclare Paper Mill remained open until the mill closed in 1950. The line itself was officially closed on 3 July 1950 by the Ulster Transport Authority, who had acquired it by then.

Ballyboley Junction – Doagh

Passenger service withdrawn	1st October 1930	*Stations closed*	*Date*
Distance	5.75 miles	Ballyboley Junction *	1st February 1933
Company	Northern Counties Committee	Ballynure **	1st October 1930
		Ballyclare	1st October 1930
		Doagh	1st October 1930

Ballyclare narrow gauge station, looking south. This was the terminus station until the Ballymena & Larne Railway extended the branch south to Doagh in 1884.

* Opened as Ballyclare Junction and renamed in 1889.   ** Opened by May 1879.

With just under two months of passenger services to go until closure, NCC locomotive No. 109 stands at Doagh with the 7.10 p.m. service to Ballyboley on 9 August 1930. Doagh retained a goods service until 1944

Much of the earlier history of the Ballymena & Larne Railway has been recounted in the previous section. The Ballyboley Junction to Ballyclare and Ballyclare Paper Mill line opened to goods traffic on 1 September 1877 with passenger traffic commencing the following year on 24 August 1878. Among the extension railways proposed by the Ballymena & Larne Railway was an extension from Ballyclare to Doagh, authorised on 8 August 1878 with work beginning on the extension in 1883. The line was opened to goods traffic on 8 February 1884 and opened to passengers on 1 May 1884. The main traffic down the branch was to Ballyclare Paper Mill, which had its own siding. The fortunes of the branch followed that of the main route, but falling receipts on the branch led to an earlier closure to passengers, which happened on 1 October 1930. Ballyboley Junction Station remained open on the main route until the withdrawal of services on that line. Goods traffic soldiered on down to Doagh until 15 June 1944 when the Ballyclare Paper Mill to Doagh section was closed completely. The Paper Mill kept the rest of the line going, but when it closed that was the end. The Ulster Transport Authority closed the branch on 3 July 1950.

Ballymena – Parkmore and Retreat

Passenger service withdrawn	1 October 1930	*Stations closed*	*Date*
Distance	16.25 miles	Rathkenny	1 October 1930
Company	Northern Counties Committee	Clough Road	1 October 1930
		Martinstown **	1 October 1930
Stations closed	*Date*	Cross Roads ***	1 October 1930
Ballygarvey *	1 October 1930	Cargan	1 October 1930
Ballycloughan	1 October 1930	Parkmore	1 October 1930

Ballymena Station, which remains open. Rebuilt in 1904, the design of the new station paid special attention to the interchange between the broad gauge and narrow gauge lines.

* Advertised in timetables from August 1887.
** Opened as Knockanally and renamed Martinstown in April 1920.

*** Opened as Carrowcowan in 1888 and renamed Cross Roads by July 1889.

A view taken inside Ballymena Station from the broad gauge down platform.

The hills to the north of Ballymena contained iron ore, a valuable resource that was soon the attention of various mining concerns. The problem at the time was the transportation of heavy carts over very poor roads to the coast at Red Bay where the ore was loaded onto boats for shipment to England. It was decided to build a railway from the mines at Cloughcor to Milltown Pier. Built in 1873, this line was the first narrow gauge line to be opened in Ireland and its gauge of three feet soon became the adopted second Irish standard gauge. Eventually the mines became uneconomic to work and the line closed in 1876. However, there were still a number of workable mines nearer to Ballymena and despite the presence of a wire tramway to the bay, a railway line to Ballymena seemed the obvious solution. The Ballymena, Cushendall & Red Bay Railway was the first narrow gauge railway to be incorporated in Ireland on 18 July 1872. The intention was to build a freight-only 3 feet gauge line from Ballymena to the pier at Red Bay, some twenty-two and a quarter miles away. Efforts in raising capital were disappointing and as a result it was decided to start with the construction of the Ballymena to Cargan section.

This section was opened for iron ore traffic on 26 March 1875 with general goods traffic following on 1 July 1875. Meanwhile, work had started on the remainder of the line, but it never reached Cushendall or Red Bay on account of the severe gradients that would have been encountered. It was decided to terminate the line at Retreat, an isolated place some five miles from Cushendall. The line had the distinction of having the highest point on any railway in Ireland at Essathohan Siding, between Parkmore and Retreat, the summit being 1,045 feet above sea level. The line opened in two stages, to Parkmore on 1 January 1876 and to Retreat on 8 October 1876. The line served various mines along the route, being connected by long sidings. Traffic was fairly buoyant to begin with, the ore being taken to Ballymena, transhipped to the broad gauge and taken to Larne Harbour via Carrickfergus Junction. The opening of the three feet gauge Ballymena & Larne Railway's link to the BNCR station allowed a more direct route to Larne without having to change gauge.

Ballymena Station, looking towards Belfast and the narrow gauge platform, 20 June 1938.

The shed at Ballymena Station with the mixed gauge trackwork clearly visible, 20 June 1938.

However, a depression in the iron ore market in the 1880s turned the fortunes of the company. With little ore and goods traffic and no passenger traffic, things became difficult. The company investigated the possibility of upgrading the line for passenger traffic, but the £9,000 it would have cost was out of their reach. Eventually, the directors of the company had no other option but to sell the line to the Belfast & Northern Counties Railway in 1884. The BNCR upgraded the line for passenger use with services to Knockanally commencing on 5 April 1886 and to Parkmore on 27 August 1888. The isolated terminus at Retreat did not get a passenger service but remained in use for goods traffic. Deprived of its ore traffic, the line was never profitable but carried on to 1 October 1930 when the LMS NCC withdrew passenger services. Goods traffic continued for several more years until the section of line from the Rathkenny Creamery Siding to Retreat was closed completely by the LMS NCC on 10 April 1937. The remaining six miles continued to serve the Creamery Siding until eventually that too was closed on 2 June 1940.

Ballymoney – Ballycastle

Passenger service withdrawn	3 July 1950	*Stations closed*	*Date*
Distance	16.25 miles	Gracehill *	3 July 1950
Company	Northern Counties Committee	Armoy	3 July 1950
		Capecastle **	3 July 1950
		Ballycastle	3 July 1950
Stations closed	*Date*		
Ballymoney	3 July 1950	* Opened in December 1880.	
Dervock	3 July 1950	** Opened in February 1882.	
Stranocum	3 July 1950		

Ballymoney Station was another NCC station which served two gauges. This was the starting point for the Ballycastle line and waiting with the 2.55 p.m. service to Ballycastle on 10 August 1930 is narrow gauge locomotive No. 106, built in 1877 by Beyer, Peacock.

Ballymoney Station, facing Belfast, with Class W Mogul No. 100, 'Queen Elizabeth', arriving at the platform, 20 May 1950.

The small town of Ballycastle sits on the northern coast of Co. Antrim. Coal mining had been in progress there from an early date and between 1740 and 1743 there had been a 300 yard long wooden tramway in use, transporting coal to the harbour – possibly the first railed way in Ireland. However, the proposal to build a railway to Ballycastle hinged on its possible success as a seaside resort rather than mineral traffic.

NCC narrow gauge Class Q 0-6-0T No. 106 stands at Ballymoney Station. Originally built for the Ballymena & Larne Railway, this was one of the locomotives transferred to the Ballycastle line with the reopening in 1924.

An early proposal by the Belfast & Northern Counties Railway in 1863 had come to nothing, but another scheme was promoted in 1876. This involved a 3 feet gauge railway starting from the BNCR station at Ballymoney, running the sixteen and a quarter miles north-east to Ballycastle.

NCC narrow gauge S Class No. 43 arrives at Ballymoney with the 10.40 a.m. service from Ballycastle, 18 April 1948. Built by the NCC in 1920, the locomotive was a 2 cylinder von Borries compound, with one high-pressure cylinder on one side of the locomotive and a slightly larger low-pressure cylinder on the other. No. 43 survived until 1954.

Construction of the Ballycastle Railway started in December 1878 and it was hoped to have the line open in readiness for the summer traffic of 1880. However, the inspecting officer from the Board of Trade was unhappy with the cheap way the line had been built and didn't give permission for it to open until 18 October 1880, by which time the defects had been corrected.

Dervock Station on the Ballycastle line. This was the first station on the line, some four and a half miles from Ballymoney. Pictured on 20 May 1950, the whole line was destined for closure two months later.

From the start the railway was always in financial difficulties, despite attempts at various economies. By 1922 the Railway Commission had become aware of the Ballycastle Railway's difficulties and recommended its absorption by the NCC. However, a large loss at the end of 1923 spelled the end of the railway.

Armoy Station, facing Ballycastle, 20 May 1950.

At a meeting of the Board on 21 January 1924 it was decided to close the line. On 8 February the shareholders consented to the closure and this happened on 24 March 1924.

But this closure was by no means the end of the story. The railway approached the new Northern Ireland government for assistance, but they were not prepared to help as they had other matters to deal with. So the only other options available were to either try and sell the line as a going concern or sell it for scrap.

NCC S Class No. 43 takes on water at Ballycastle, 18 April 1948. Standing at the platform are carriages Nos. 352 and 353. These carriages were among four specially built for the Ballymena and Larne boat trains in 1928. Complete with lavatories and corridor connections, they offered higher levels of comfort to any other narrow gauge carriages in the country. They were transferred to the Ballycastle line in 1933 after the boat trains were discontinued.

The neighbouring Northern Counties Committee were approached and they offered £10,000. Obviously disappointed with the offer, the Board asked for more and other shareholders lobbied the NCC to increase their offer, which eventually they did. So the Ballycastle Railway was sold to the LMS NCC for £12,500 on 4 May 1924.

NCC Q Class No. 106, ready to depart Ballycastle with the 1.20 p.m. service to Ballymoney, 10 August 1930. Note the somersault signal which was a common feature of the NCC system.

Services did not recommence immediately as the new owners had a backlog of maintenance to catch up with as well as re-equipping the line with rolling stock transferred from the NCC's other narrow gauge lines. The railway reopened on 11 August 1924, although legal title to the line did not come about until 7 August 1925.

Locomotive No. 43 with coaches Nos. 352 and 353 at Ballycastle, forming the 2.15 p.m. service to Ballymoney, 18 April 1948. The line closed completely two years later.

The new owners managed to keep the line running economically to the extent that it was the last of the NCC narrow gauge lines to close. The end finally came on 3 July 1950 when the Ulster Transport Authority closed the line completely.

Portrush – Giant's Causeway

Passenger service withdrawn	1 October 1949
Distance	9.25 miles
Company	Giant's Causeway, Portrush & Bush Valley Tramway

Stations closed	*Date*
Portrush	1 October 1949
Portrush Post Office	1 October 1949
Royal Portrush Golf Club	1 October 1949
Ballymoney Road	1 October 1949
White Rocks	1 October 1949
Dunluce Castle	1 October 1949

Stations closed	*Date*
Portballintrae	1 October 1949
Gortnee	1 October 1949
Stanalane	1 October 1949
Bushmills	1 October 1949
Bushmills Market Yard	1890
Bushfoot Golf Links	1 October 1949
Bushfoot Strand	1 October 1949
Runkerry	1 October 1949
Giant's Causeway	1 October 1949

A steam-hauled tram making its way through the streets of Portrush. Four 0-4-0 vertical boiler tram engines were supplied to the Giant's Causeway by the firm of Wilkinson. Steam working ceased in 1916.

The tram station at Bushmills.

With the coming of the railway to Portrush in 1855, the small town of Bushmills, some six miles to the east, was keen to be connected to the railway system. The Ballymena, Ballymoney, Coleraine & Portrush Junction Railway, and its successor, the Belfast & Northern Counties Railway, had on numerous occasions thought about extending the line to Bushmills and on through to the Giant's Causeway about ten miles east of Portrush. However, the cost of laying a broad gauge line along this route and cutting through basalt was considered prohibitively expensive and nothing was done.

Walkmills hydroelectric power station supplied the traction current for the Giant's Causeway tramway, although a supplementary diesel generator at Portrush Depot assisted in busy periods. This photograph was taken on 15 July 1933.

A couple of abortive schemes were proposed in the late 1870s to connect Portrush, Bushmills and the Giant's Causeway by a tramway running along the public road. However, it was the 1880 proposal of the Giant's Causeway, Portrush & Bush Valley Tramway Company that came to fruition. Built to a gauge of 3 feet, chosen because of a proposed line to Dervock on the Ballycastle Railway and possible through running, the method of propulsion used on this tramway was unique. The proposal was to use electric traction from power generated at a hydroelectric generating station using a waterfall near Bushmills. An additional steam powered generating plant was built at Portrush to supplement the supply.

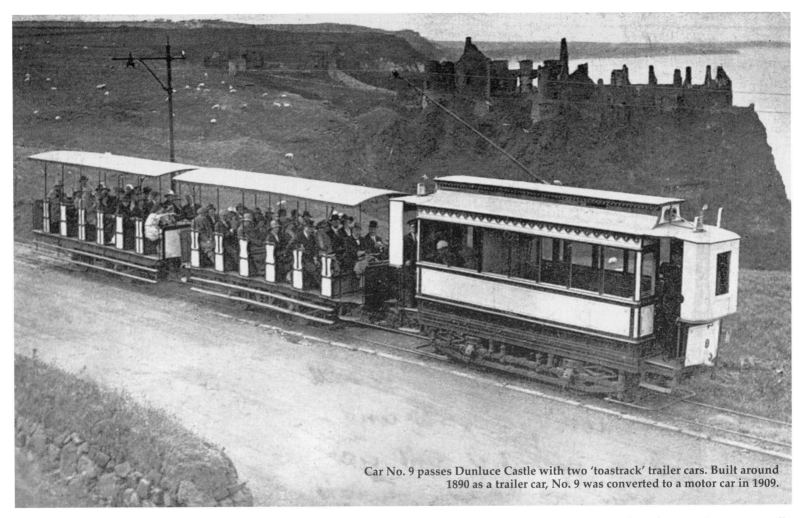

Car No. 9 passes Dunluce Castle with two 'toastrack' trailer cars. Built around 1890 as a trailer car, No. 9 was converted to a motor car in 1909.

During the construction of the line, numerous experiments were carried out to find the best way of transmitting power along the route. It was eventually decided to use the third rail system at 250 volts D.C. The third rail was actually some 22 inches away from the running rails on the north side of the track and some 17 inches above the track. A metal brush on the side of the tramcar picked up the current and the return circuit was via the wheels and running rails.

The Victoria Jubilee Bridge, built in 1887, was on the Bushmills to Giant's Causeway section of the tramway.

The section between Portrush Station and Bushmills was opened on 29 January 1883, although steam traction was used initially pending the completion of electrical experiments. A branch to Portrush Harbour was also built which used a third rail laid along the BNCR harbour branch to form a mixed gauge route to the harbour for goods traffic, opening later that year.

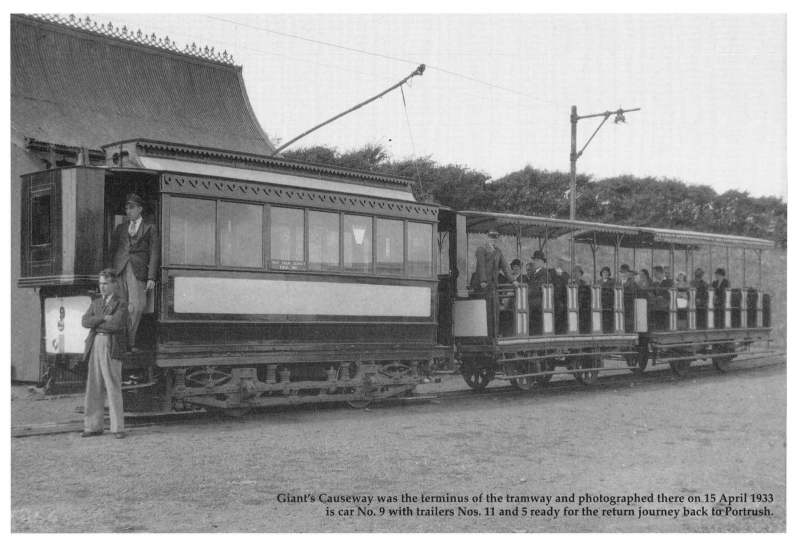

Giant's Causeway was the terminus of the tramway and photographed there on 15 April 1933 is car No. 9 with trailers Nos. 11 and 5 ready for the return journey back to Portrush.

The electric service officially commenced on 28 September 1883, but regular electric services didn't start until November due to continuing electrical problems. The steam engines were still used to work the trains on the street sections between the tram depot and Portrush Station and at Bushmills.

Car No. 9 rests in a siding, trolley down, with two trailers at the Giant's Causeway terminus, 10 August 1930.

Work on the extension of the line to the Giant's Causeway commenced in 1886, the extension opening the following year on 1 July. The little used mixed gauge harbour branch was closed a month earlier, although the broad gauge part remained open until 1949. The terminus was actually about a mile short of the Causeway entrance, no doubt due to the vested interests of local hoteliers and the operators of horse-drawn carriages.

Although the tramway closed in 1949, Portrush still plays a long-standing part in the remaining railway network. The town's station opened on 7 November 1855 on the line from Coleraine to Portrush Harbour. This line is still open to Portrush, although the spur to the harbour was closed by the UTA in 1949.

With the opening of the extension, the former end of the line at Bushmills Market Yard was bypassed. This spur only lasted a few more years before closing in 1890. An accident in 1895 put an end the to the third rail system when an unfortunate cyclist fell off his bicycle and was thrown against the third rail. He later died. The following Board of Trade investigation resulted in the suspension of electric services until the third rail was either boxed in or raised to a position eight feet above the ground. The solution adopted was to equip the line with an overhead wire. The installation of the overhead equipment and conversion of the tramcars to the trolley system was carried out and overhead workings began on 26 July 1899. The opportunity was also taken to extend electric services to Portrush Station. In 1900 the supply voltage was increased to 550 volts D.C.

Originally Portrush Station had only one platform, but in 1893 it was rebuilt in impressive mock-Tudor style and given three 600 feet long platforms. It also had a 6,000 feet square booking hall and an adjoining café which could cater for 300. The main building still stands, although the facilities are now much reduced.

For the next forty odd years the tramway serviced the tourist industry, but was never very profitable as a bad summer would seriously affect finances. The company did try to sell the line unsuccessfully on a few occasions, firstly to the Midland Railway in 1903 and later to the LMS NCC several times in the 1920s. However, the line continued earning a meagre living until the outbreak of the Second World War. During this period, a large number of American servicemen were stationed in Northern Ireland, many of whom visited the Causeway, and as a result a special winter service was introduced in 1940 and lasted until 1947.

NCC U2 Class 4-4-0 No. 74 stands at Portrush Station with the 8.00 a.m. service to Belfast, 10 August 1930. Built by the North British Locomotive Company in 1924, No. 74 was named 'Dunluce Castle' in 1931.

Despite the temporary upturn of business during the war, falling receipts and the somewhat decrepit infrastructure, which was badly in need of replacement, prompted the owners to again seek a buyer for the tramway. This time they had in mind the Ulster Transport Authority who predictably declined the offer. A distinct lack of interest by the government of Northern Ireland forced the company to the conclusion that they would have to close the line.

UTA Class W Mogul No. 91, 'The Bush', at Portrush with the 2.00 p.m. Coleraine service, August 1953.

The last tram ran on 30 September 1949, although this is not quite the end of the story. In 1996 a group of enthusiasts formed a company to reopen a two-mile section of the tramway between Bushmills and Giant's Causeway. After a long haul, the first section of the Giant's Causeway Railway opened on 16 March 2002. The preserved railway uses locomotives and carriages from the former Shane's Castle Railway that closed in 1995.

Closed passenger stations on lines still open to passenger services

Belfast – Macfin

Line/service	Date
Stations closed	
Belfast York Road	17 October 1992
Greencastle *	1 June 1916
Whitehouse (old station)	June 1906
Whitehouse (new station)	20 September 1954
Monkstown (new station) **	23 February 1981

Stations closed	Date
Monkstown (old station)	28 May 1933
Mossley (old station)	1 November 1931
Mossley (new station) ***	23 February 1981
Ballyclare Junction ****	4 December 1961
Ballyrobert Halt	January 1920
Doagh *****	29 June 1970

* Originally called Whitehouse but renamed Greencastle in 1849/50.
** Closed *c.*1959 and reopened on 4 September 1967; closed again on 23 January 1978 and reopened 1 September 1980.
*** Closed 20 September 1954 and reopened on 1 September 1980.
**** Formerly called Ballynure Road and renamed on 3 November 1884; closed in August 1875 and reopened on 1 June 1877.
***** Formerly called Ballypallady, then renamed Ballyclare & Doagh in October 1858, and again as Doagh on 3 November 1884.

York Road was the Belfast terminus and headquarters of the NCC. The station was closed in 1992 and replaced by the smaller Yorkgate Station while the Cross Harbour link was being built. The link opened in 1994 and enabled services to continue to Belfast Central.

Line/service		Stations closed	Date
	Belfast – Macfin (continued)	Andraid ****	1850
		Ballymena (old station) *****	4 December 1855
Stations closed	Date	Glarryford	2 July 1973
Templepatrick *	23 February 1981	Killagan †	2 July 1973
Dunadry	20 September 1954	Dunloy	18 October 1976
Muckamore Halt	6 May 1963	Macfin (old station)	1867
Oriel Lodge Racecourse **	1948	Macfin (new station)	20th September 1954
Drumsough ***	18 October 1976		
Kellswater	15 March 1971		

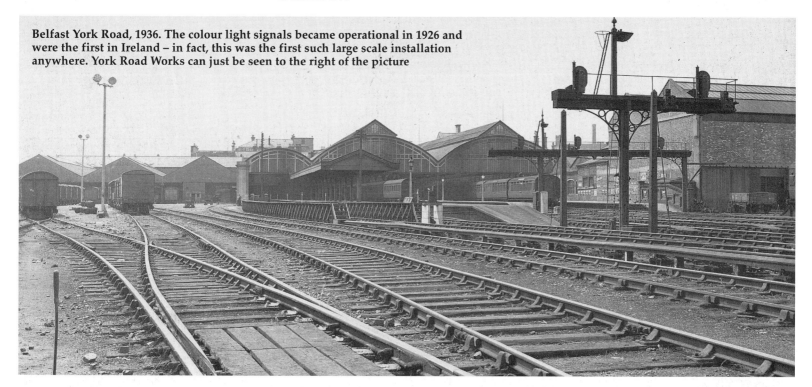

Belfast York Road, 1936. The colour light signals became operational in 1926 and were the first in Ireland – in fact, this was the first such large scale installation anywhere. York Road Works can just be seen to the right of the picture

* Closed on 20 September 1954 and reopened on 1 September 1980.
** Also called Niblock Crossing Racecourse Platform.
*** Originally called Drumsough Junction, then renamed Cookstown Junction in November 1856, and again as Drumsough on 26 April 1976.

**** Flag Station (i.e. an unmanned request stop) with services on Wednesdays and Fridays only.
***** Old Belfast and Ballymena terminus which was closed when the current station opened on the extension to Coleraine.
† Formerly called Bellaghy and renamed in January 1876.

NCC A1 Class 4-4-0 No. 58 stands at Belfast York Road. Built by the NCC as Class A compound locomotive No. 17 in 1907, it was renumbered in 1927 and rebuilt as a simple locomotive in 1934.

Macfin Station, looking south, 1937. The Derry Central line is on the right.

Line/service		**Bleach Green Junction – Larne**		Stations closed	Date
				Eden Halt	9 May 1977
Stations closed			Date	Kilroot	9 May 1977
Bleach Green Halt *			9 May 1977	Whitehead (first station)	1 June 1864
Mount Halt **			8 May 1972	Whitehead (second station)	June 1877
Carrickfergus (old station)			1862	Larne ****	23 June 1974
Barn Halt ***			9 May 1977	Larne Harbour (old station) *****	c.1890

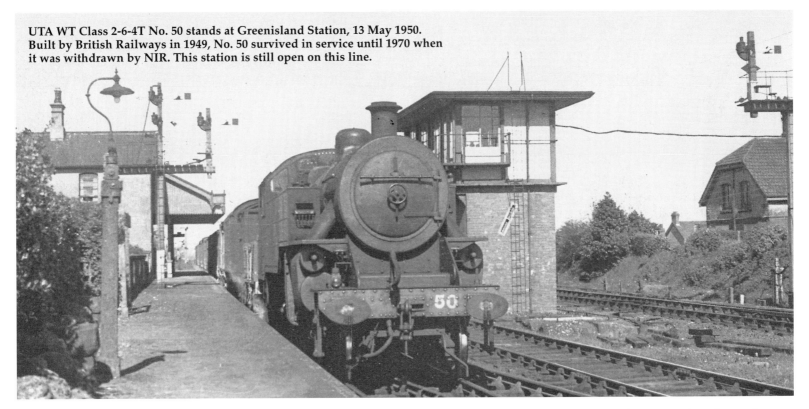

UTA WT Class 2-6-4T No. 50 stands at Greenisland Station, 13 May 1950. Built by British Railways in 1949, No. 50 survived in service until 1970 when it was withdrawn by NIR. This station is still open on this line.

* Closed on 23 October 1932 and reopened 22 January 1934 on a new site.
** Closed on 1 October 1930, reopening on 1 July 1946 as Courtaulds' Platform and renamed Mount on 7 October 1946.
*** Closed on 1 June 1931 and reopened c.1942.

**** Closed on 23 June 1974 due to deviation works and a new Larne Town Station opened on the new route.
***** Old station replaced by a new Larne Harbour Station.

Greenisland Station, 13 May 1950. Trains to and from the Antrim direction had to reverse here until 1934 when the LMS NCC built the 'Loop Line'. This allowed these trains to continue without reversal and bypassed Greenisland, leaving it solely on the Larne line.

Another WT Class 2-6-4T locomotive, this time No. 2, at Larne Station
with the 5.35 p.m. Belfast to Larne Harbour service, 22 April 1948.

Line/service	**Knockmore Junction – Antrim**	Stations closed	Date
		Meeting House Halt	12 September 1960
Stations closed	Date	Legatiriff Halt	1960
Brookmount	1960	Aldergrove	1960
Brookhill Halt	1960	Millar's Bridge Halt	12 September 1960

NCC Class V 0-6-0 locomotive No. 14 with a southbound goods service at Antrim Station, 26 June 1937. This station remains open.